Pastor Elaine,

So thankful
for you & who
you are in the

Kingdom
MP

CALLED Ministry

5942 Bridlewood Lane

Charlotte, NC 28215

bpeacock888@gmail.com

Preface

The book of Psalms is considered the hymnbook of the Bible. Each Psalm provides a source of praise, prayer and worship, allowing the "created" to meet and converse with the "Creator." The Psalms were written to be read, recited and sung to God as an act of worship.

The book of Psalms is divided into five sections. Each section concludes with a doxology. Psalm 119, book five, is a wisdom psalm that probes life's mysteries. This Psalm teaches us about ourselves and God.

In this journal you will find two translations of each scripture from Psalm 119. The references are written in the King James Version and the New Living Translation. Even though they are the same verses, the Word may speak to you differently based upon the translation.

Prayerfully journal as the Spirit speaks to you through the passage(s) or from other directions and insight. Just flow in His presence and reflect.

PSALM 119:1

"Blessed are the undefiled in the way, who walk in the law of the LORD *(KJV)."*

"Joyful are people of integrity, who follow the instructions of the LORD *(NLT)."*

Journal Notes

_____

_____

_____

_____

_____

_____

_____

_____

_____

_____

_____

PSALM 119:2

"Blessed are they that keep his testimonies, and that seek him with the whole heart (KJV)."

"Joyful are those who obey his laws and search for him with all their hearts (NLT)."

Journal Notes

_____

_____

_____

_____

_____

_____

_____

_____

_____

_____

_____

_____

PSALM 119:3

"They also do no iniquity: they walk in his ways *(KJV).***"**

"They do not compromise with evil, and they walk only in his paths *(NLT).***"**

Journal Notes

_____

_____

_____

_____

_____

_____

_____

_____

_____

_____

_____

PSALM 119:4

"Thou has commanded us to keep thy precepts diligently (KJV)."

"You have charged us to keep your commandments carefully (NLT)."

Journal Notes

_____

_____

_____

_____

_____

_____

_____

_____

_____

_____

_____

PSALM 119:5

"O that my ways were directed to keep thy statutes *(KJV)***!"**

"Oh, that my actions would consistently reflect your decrees *(NLT)***!"**

Journal Notes

_____

_____

_____

_____

_____

_____

_____

_____

_____

_____

_____

PSALM 119:6

"Then shall I not be ashamed, when I have respect unto all thy commandments (KJV)."

"Then I will not be ashamed when I compare my life with your commands (NLT)."

Journal Notes

PSALM 119:7

"I will praise thee with uprightness of heart, when I shall have learned thy righteous judgments (KJV)."

"As I learn your righteous regulations, I will thank you by living as I should (NLT)!"

Journal Notes

_____

_____

_____

_____

_____

_____

_____

_____

_____

_____

PSALM 119:8

"I will keep thy statutes: O forsake me not utterly (KJV)*."*

"I will obey your decrees. Please don't give up on me (NLT)*!"*

Journal Notes

_____

_____

_____

_____

_____

_____

_____

_____

_____

_____

_____

PSALM 119:9

"Wherewithal shall a young man cleanse his way? By taking heed thereto according to thy word (KJV)."

"How can a young person stay pure? By obeying your word (NLT)."

Journal Notes

_____

_____

_____

_____

_____

_____

_____

_____

_____

_____

_____

PSALM 119:10

"With my whole heart have I sought thee: O let me not wander from thy commandments (KJV)."

"I have tried hard to find you— don't let me wander from your commands (NLT)."

Journal Notes

_____

_____

_____

_____

_____

_____

_____

_____

_____

_____

PSALM 119:11

"Thy word have I hid in mine heart, that I might not sin against thee (KJV)."

"I have hidden your word in my heart, that I might not sin against you (NLT)."

Journal Notes

_____

_____

_____

_____

_____

_____

_____

_____

_____

_____

_____

PSALM 119:12

"Blessed art thou, O LORD: teach me thy statutes (KJV)."

"I praise you, O LORD; teach me your decrees (NLT)."

Journal Notes

_____

_____

_____

_____

_____

_____

_____

_____

_____

_____

_____

PSALM 119:13

"With my lips have I declared all the judgments of thy mouth (KJV).**"**

"I have recited aloud all the regulations you have given us (NLT).**"**

Journal Notes

_____

_____

_____

_____

_____

_____

_____

_____

_____

_____

_____

PSALM 119:14

"I have rejoiced in the way of thy testimonies, as much as in all riches (KJV)."

"I have rejoiced in your laws as much as in riches (NLT)."

Journal Notes

_____

_____

_____

_____

_____

_____

_____

_____

_____

_____

PSALM 119:15

"I will meditate in thy precepts, and have respect unto thy ways (KJV)."

"I will study your commandments and reflect on your ways (NLT)."

Journal Notes

_____

_____

_____

_____

_____

_____

_____

_____

_____

_____

_____

PSALM 119:16

"I will delight myself in thy statutes: I will not forget thy word (KJV)."

"I will delight in your decrees and not forget your word (NLT)."

Journal Notes

_____

_____

_____

_____

_____

_____

_____

_____

_____

_____

PSALM 119:17

"Deal bountifully with thy servant, that I may live, and keep thy word (KJV)."

"Be good to your servant, that I may live and obey your word (NLT)."

Journal Notes

_____

_____

_____

_____

_____

_____

_____

_____

_____

_____

PSALM 119:18

"Open thou mine eyes, that I may behold wondrous things out of thy law (KJV)."

"Open my eyes to see the wonderful truths in your instructions (NLT)."

Journal Notes

_____

_____

_____

_____

_____

_____

_____

_____

_____

_____

PSALM 119:19

"I am a stranger in the earth: hide not thy commandments from me (KJV)**."**

"I am only a foreigner in the land. Don't hide your commands from me (NLT)**!"**

Journal Notes

_____

_____

_____

_____

_____

_____

_____

_____

_____

_____

PSALM 119:20

"My soul breaketh for the longing that it hath unto thy judgments at all times (KJV)."

"I am always overwhelmed with a desire for your regulations (NLT)."

Journal Notes

_____

_____

_____

_____

_____

_____

_____

_____

_____

_____

_____

PSALM 119:21

"Thou hast rebuked the proud that are cursed, which do err from thy commandments (KJV)."

"You rebuke the arrogant; those who wander from your commands are cursed (NLT)."

Journal Notes

_____

_____

_____

_____

_____

_____

_____

_____

_____

_____

_____

PSALM 119:22

"Remove from me reproach and contempt; for I have kept thy testimonies (KJV)."

"Don't let them scorn and insult me, for I have obeyed your laws (NLT)."

Journal Notes

_____

_____

_____

_____

_____

_____

_____

_____

_____

_____

PSALM 119:23

"Princes also did sit and speak against me: but thy servant did meditate in thy statutes (KJV)."

"Even princes sit and speak against me, but I will meditate on your decrees (NLT)."

Journal Notes

_____

_____

_____

_____

_____

_____

_____

_____

_____

_____

PSALM 119:24

"Thy testimonies also are my delight and my counselors (KJV)."

"Your laws please me; they give me wise advice (NLT)."

<u>Journal Notes</u>

_____

_____

_____

_____

_____

_____

_____

_____

_____

_____

PSALM 119:25

"My soul cleaveth unto the dust: quicken thou me according to thy word (KJV)."

"I lie in the dust; revive me by your word (NLT)."

Journal Notes

_____

_____

_____

_____

_____

_____

_____

_____

_____

_____

PSALM 119:26

"I have declared my ways, and thou heardest me: teach me thy statutes (KJV)."

"I told you my plans, and you answered. Now teach me your decrees (NLT)."

Journal Notes

_____

_____

_____

_____

_____

_____

_____

_____

_____

_____

PSALM 119:27

"Make me to understand the way of thy precepts: so shall I talk of thy wondrous works (KJV)."

"Help me understand the meaning of your commandments, and I will meditate on your wonderful deeds (NLT)."

<u>Journal Notes</u>

_____

_____

_____

_____

_____

_____

_____

_____

_____

PSALM 119:28

"*My soul melteth for heaviness: strengthen thou me according unto thy word* (KJV)."

"*I weep with sorrow; encourage me by your word* (NLT)."

Journal Notes

_____

_____

_____

_____

_____

_____

_____

_____

_____

_____

PSALM 119:29

"Remove from me the way of lying: and grant me thy law graciously (KJV)."

"Keep me from lying to myself; give me the privilege of knowing your instructions (NLT)."

Journal Notes

_____

_____

_____

_____

_____

_____

_____

_____

_____

_____

PSALM 119:30

"I have chosen the way of truth: thy judgments have I laid before me (KJV)."

"I have chosen to be faithful; I have determined to live by your regulations (NLT)."

Journal Notes

_____

_____

_____

_____

_____

_____

_____

_____

_____

_____

_____

PSALM 119:31

"I have stuck unto thy testimonies: O LORD, put me not to shame (KJV)."

"I cling to your laws. LORD, don't let me be put to shame (NLT)!"

Journal Notes

_____

_____

_____

_____

_____

_____

_____

_____

_____

_____

PSALM 119:32

"I will run the way of thy commandments, when thou shalt enlarge my heart (KJV)."

"I will pursue your commands, for you expand my understanding (NLT)."

Journal Notes

_____

_____

_____

_____

_____

_____

_____

_____

_____

_____

_____

PSALM 119:33

"Teach me, O LORD, the way of thy statutes; and I shall keep it unto the end (KJV)*."*

"Teach me your decrees, O LORD; I will keep them to the end (NLT)*."*

Journal Notes

_____

_____

_____

_____

_____

_____

_____

_____

_____

_____

PSALM 119:34

"Give me understanding, and I shall keep thy law; yea, I shall observe it with my whole heart (KJV)."

"Give me understanding and I will obey your instructions; I will put them into practice with all my heart (NLT)."

Journal Notes

_____

_____

_____

_____

_____

_____

_____

_____

_____

_____

PSALM 119:35

"Make me to go in the path of thy commandments; for therein do I delight (KJV)."

"Make me walk along the path of your commands, for that is where my happiness is found (NLT)."

Journal Notes

_____

_____

_____

_____

_____

_____

_____

_____

_____

_____

PSALM 119:36

"Incline my heart unto thy testimonies, and not to covetousness (KJV)."

"Give me an eagerness for your laws rather than a love for money (NLT)!"

Journal Notes

_____

_____

_____

_____

_____

_____

_____

_____

_____

_____

PSALM 119:37

"Turn away mine eyes from beholding vanity; and quicken thou me in thy way (KJV)."

"Turn my eyes from worthless things, and give me life through your word (NLT)."

Journal Notes

_____

_____

_____

_____

_____

_____

_____

_____

_____

_____

_____

PSALM 119:38

"Stablish thy word unto thy servant, who is devoted to thy fear (KJV)."

"Reassure me of your promise, made to those who fear you (NLT)."

Journal Notes

_____

_____

_____

_____

_____

_____

_____

_____

_____

_____

PSALM 119:39

"Turn away my reproach which I fear: for thy judgments are good (KJV)."

"Help me abandon my shameful ways; for your regulations are good (NLT)."

Journal Notes

_____

_____

_____

_____

_____

_____

_____

_____

_____

_____

PSALM 119:40

"Behold, I have longed after thy precepts: quicken me in thy righteousness (KJV)."

"I long to obey your commandments! Renew my life with your goodness (NLT)."

Journal Notes

_____

_____

_____

_____

_____

_____

_____

_____

_____

_____

PSALM 119:41

"Let thy mercies come also unto me, O LORD, even thy salvation, according to thy word (KJV)."

"LORD, give me your unfailing love, the salvation that you promised me (NLT)."

Journal Notes

_____

_____

_____

_____

_____

_____

_____

_____

_____

_____

PSALM 119:42

"So shall I have wherewith to answer him that reproacheth me: for I trust in thy word (KJV)."

"Then I can answer those who taunt me, for I trust in your word (NLT)."

Journal Notes

_____

_____

_____

_____

_____

_____

_____

_____

_____

_____

PSALM 119:43

"And take not the word of truth utterly out of my mouth; for I have hoped in thy judgments (KJV)."

"Do not snatch your word of truth from me, for your regulations are my only hope (NLT)."

Journal Notes

_____

_____

_____

_____

_____

_____

_____

_____

_____

PSALM 119:44

"So shall I keep thy law continually forever and ever (KJV).*"*

"I will keep on obeying your instructions forever and ever (NLT).*"*

Journal Notes

_____

_____

_____

_____

_____

_____

_____

_____

_____

_____

PSALM 119:45

"And I will walk at liberty: for I seek thy precepts (KJV)."

"I will walk in freedom, for I have devoted myself to your commandments (NLT)."

Journal Notes

_____

_____

_____

_____

_____

_____

_____

_____

_____

_____

PSALM 119:46

"I will speak of thy testimonies also before kings, and will not be ashamed (KJV)."

"I will speak to kings about your laws, and I will not be ashamed (NLT)."

Journal Notes

_____

_____

_____

_____

_____

_____

_____

_____

_____

_____

PSALM 119:47

"And I will delight myself in thy command-ments, which I have loved (KJV)."

"How I delight in your commands! How I love them (NLT)!"

Journal Notes

_____

_____

_____

_____

_____

_____

_____

_____

_____

_____

PSALM 119:48

"My hands also will I lift up unto thy commandments, which I have loved; and I will meditate in thy statutes (KJV)."

"I honor and love your commands. I meditate on your decrees (NLT)."

Journal Notes

_____

_____

_____

_____

_____

_____

_____

_____

_____

PSALM 119:49

"Remember the word unto thy servant, upon which thou hast caused me to hope (KJV)."

"Remember your promise to me; it is my only hope (NLT)."

<u>Journal Notes</u>

_____

_____

_____

_____

_____

_____

_____

_____

_____

_____

PSALM 119:50

"This is my comfort in my affliction: for thy word hath quickened me (KJV)."

"Your promise revives me; it comforts me in all my troubles (NLT)."

Journal Notes

_____

_____

_____

_____

_____

_____

_____

_____

_____

_____

PSALM 119:51

"The proud have had me greatly in derision: yet have I not declined from thy law (KJV)."

"The proud hold me in utter contempt, but I do not turn away from your instructions (NLT)."

Journal Notes

_____

_____

_____

_____

_____

_____

_____

_____

_____

_____

_____

PSALM 119:52

"I remembered thy judgments of old, O LORD; and have comforted myself (KJV)."

"I meditate on your age-old regulations; O LORD, they comfort me (NLT)."

Journal Notes

_____

_____

_____

_____

_____

_____

_____

_____

_____

_____

PSALM 119:53

"Horror hath taken hold upon me because of the wicked that forsake thy law (KJV)."

"I become furious with the wicked, because they reject your instructions (NLT)."

Journal Notes

_____

_____

_____

_____

_____

_____

_____

_____

_____

_____

PSALM 119:54

"Thy statutes have been my songs in the house of my pilgrimage (KJV)."

"Your decrees have been the theme of my songs wherever I have lived (NLT)."

Journal Notes

_____

_____

_____

_____

_____

_____

_____

_____

_____

_____

PSALM 119:55

"I have remembered thy name, O LORD, in the night, and have kept thy law (KJV)."

"I reflect at night on who you are, O LORD; therefore, I obey your instructions (NLT)."

Journal Notes

_____

_____

_____

_____

_____

_____

_____

_____

_____

_____

PSALM 119:56

"This I had, because I kept thy precepts (KJV)."

"This is how I spend my life: obeying your commandments (NLT)."

Journal Notes

_____

_____

_____

_____

_____

_____

_____

_____

_____

_____

PSALM 119:57

"Thou art my portion, O LORD: I have said that I would keep thy words (KJV)."

"LORD, you are mine! I promise to obey your words (NLT)!"

Journal Notes

_____

_____

_____

_____

_____

_____

_____

_____

_____

_____

PSALM 119:58

"I intreated thy favour with my whole heart: be merciful unto me according to thy word (KJV)."

"With all my heart I want your blessings. Be merciful as you promised (NLT)."

Journal Notes

_____

_____

_____

_____

_____

_____

_____

_____

_____

_____

PSALM 119:59

"I thought on my ways, and turned my feet unto thy testimonies (KJV)."

"I pondered the direction of my life, and I turned to follow your laws (NLT)."

Journal Notes

_____

_____

_____

_____

_____

_____

_____

_____

_____

_____

PSALM 119:60

"I made haste, and delayed not to keep thy commandments (KJV)."

"I will hurry, without delay, to obey your commands (NLT)."

Journal Notes

_____

_____

_____

_____

_____

_____

_____

_____

_____

_____

PSALM 119:61

"The bands of the wicked have robbed me: but I have not forgotten thy law (KJV)."

"Evil people try to drag me into sin, but I am firmly anchored to your instructions (NLT)."

Journal Notes

_____

_____

_____

_____

_____

_____

_____

_____

_____

_____

_____

PSALM 119:62

"At midnight I will rise to give thanks unto thee because of thy righteous judgments (KJV)."

"I rise at midnight to thank you for your just regulations (NLT)."

Journal Notes

_____

_____

_____

_____

_____

_____

_____

_____

_____

_____

_____

_____

PSALM 119:63

"I am a companion of all them that fear thee, and of them that keep thy precepts (KJV)."

"I am a friend to anyone who fears you - anyone who obeys your commandments (NLT)."

Journal Notes

_____

_____

_____

_____

_____

_____

_____

_____

_____

PSALM 119:64

"The earth, O LORD, is full of thy mercy: teach me thy statutes (KJV)."

"O LORD, your unfailing love fills the earth; teach me your decrees (NLT)."

Journal Notes

_____

_____

_____

_____

_____

_____

_____

_____

_____

_____

_____

PSALM 119:65

"Thou hast dealt well with thy servant, O LORD, according unto thy word (KJV)."

"You have done many good things for me, LORD, just as you promised (NLT)."

Journal Notes

PSALM 119:66

"Teach me good judgment and knowledge: for I have believed thy commandments (KJV)."

"I believe in your commands; now teach me good judgment and knowledge (NLT)."

Journal Notes

_____

_____

_____

_____

_____

_____

_____

_____

_____

_____

_____

PSALM 119:67

"Before I was afflicted I went astray: but now have I kept thy word (KJV)."

"I used to wander off until you disciplined me; but now I closely follow your word (NLT)."

Journal Notes

_____

_____

_____

_____

_____

_____

_____

_____

_____

_____

_____

PSALM 119:68

"Thou art good, and doest good; teach me thy statutes (KJV)."

"You are good and do only good; teach me your decrees (NLT)."

Journal Notes

_____

_____

_____

_____

_____

_____

_____

_____

_____

_____

_____

PSALM 119:69

"The proud have forged a lie against me: but I will keep thy precepts with my whole heart (KJV)."

"Arrogant people smear me with lies, but in truth I obey your commandments with all my heart (NLT)."

Journal Notes

_____

_____

_____

_____

_____

_____

_____

_____

_____

_____

PSALM 119:70

"Their heart is as fat as grease; but I delight in thy law (KJV)."

"Their hearts are dull and stupid, but I delight in your instructions (NLT)."

Journal Notes

_____

_____

_____

_____

_____

_____

_____

_____

_____

_____

PSALM 119:71

"It is good for me that I have been afflicted; that I might learn thy statutes (KJV)."

"My suffering was good for me, for it taught me to pay attention to your decrees (NLT)."

Journal Notes

_____

_____

_____

_____

_____

_____

_____

_____

_____

_____

PSALM 119:72

"The law of thy mouth is better unto me than thousands of gold and silver (KJV)."

"Your instructions are more valuable to me than millions in gold and silver (NLT)."

Journal Notes

_____

_____

_____

_____

_____

_____

_____

_____

_____

_____

PSALM 119:73

"Thy hands have made me and fashioned me: give me understanding, that I may learn thy commandments (KJV)."

"You made me; you created me. Now give me the sense to follow your commands (NLT)."

Journal Notes

_____

_____

_____

_____

_____

_____

_____

_____

_____

PSALM 119:74

"They that fear thee will be glad when they see me; because I have hoped in thy word (KJV)."

"May all who fear you find in me a cause for joy, for I have put my hope in your word (NLT)."

Journal Notes

_____

_____

_____

_____

_____

_____

_____

_____

_____

PSALM 119:75

"I know, O LORD, that thy judgments are right, and that thou in faithfulness hast afflicted me (KJV)."

"I know O LORD that your regulations are fair; you disciplined me because I needed it (NLT)."

Journal Notes

_____

_____

_____

_____

_____

_____

_____

_____

_____

_____

_____

PSALM 119:76

"Let, I pray thee, thy merciful kindness be for my comfort, according to thy word unto thy servant (KJV)."

"Now let your unfailing love comfort me, just as you promised me, your servant (NLT)."

Journal Notes

_____

_____

_____

_____

_____

_____

_____

_____

_____

_____

PSALM 119:77

"Let thy tender mercies come unto me, that I may live: for thy law is my delight (KJV)**."**

"Surround me with your tender mercies so I may live, for your instructions are my delight (NLT)**."**

<u>Journal Notes</u>

_____

_____

_____

_____

_____

_____

_____

_____

_____

_____

PSALM 119:78

"Let the proud be ashamed; for they dealt perversely with me without a cause: but I will meditate in thy precepts (KJV)."

"Bring disgrace upon the arrogant people who lied about me; meanwhile, I will concentrate on your commandments (NLT)."

<u>Journal Notes</u>

_____

_____

_____

_____

_____

_____

_____

_____

_____

_____

PSALM 119:79

"Let those that fear thee turn unto me, and those that have known thy testimonies *(KJV).***"**

"Let me be united with all who fear you, with those who know your laws *(NLT).***"**

<u>Journal Notes</u>

_____

_____

_____

_____

_____

_____

_____

_____

_____

PSALM 119:80

"Let my heart be sound in thy statutes; that I be not ashamed (KJV)."

"May I be blameless in keeping your decrees; then I will never be ashamed (NLT)."

Journal Notes

PSALM 119:81

"My soul fainteth for thy salvation: but I hope in thy word (KJV)."

"I am worn out waiting for your rescue, but I have put my hope in your word (NLT)."

Journal Notes

_____

_____

_____

_____

_____

_____

_____

_____

_____

_____

_____

PSALM 119:82

"Mine eyes fail for thy word, saying, When wilt thou comfort me (KJV)?"

"My eyes are straining to see your promises come true. When will you comfort me (NLT)?"

Journal Notes

_____

_____

_____

_____

_____

_____

_____

_____

_____

_____

_____

PSALM 119:83

"For I am become like a bottle in the smoke; yet do I not forget thy statutes (KJV)."

"I am shriveled like a wineskin in the smoke, but I have not forgotten to obey your decrees (NLT)."

Journal Notes

_____

_____

_____

_____

_____

_____

_____

_____

_____

_____

PSALM 119:84

"How many are the days of thy servant? When wilt thou execute judgment on them that persecute me (KJV)?"

"How long must I wait? When will you punish those who persecute me (NLT)?"

Journal Notes

_____

_____

_____

_____

_____

_____

_____

_____

_____

_____

PSALM 119:85

"The proud have digged pits for me, which are not after thy law (KJV)."

"These arrogant people who hate your instructions have dug deep pits to trap me (NLT)."

Journal Notes

_____

_____

_____

_____

_____

_____

_____

_____

_____

_____

PSALM 119:86

"All thy commandments are faithful: they persecute me wrongfully; help thou me (KJV)."

"All your commands are trustworthy. Protect me from those who hunt me down without cause (NLT)."

Journal Notes

_____

_____

_____

_____

_____

_____

_____

_____

_____

PSALM 119:87

"They had almost consumed me upon earth; but I forsook not thy precepts (KJV)."

"They almost finished me off, but I refused to abandon your commandments (NLT)."

Journal Notes

_____

_____

_____

_____

_____

_____

_____

_____

_____

_____

PSALM 119:88

"Quicken me after thy lovingkindness; so shall I keep the testimony of thy mouth (KJV)."

"In your unfailing love, spare my life; then I can continue to obey your laws (NLT)."

Journal Notes

_____

_____

_____

_____

_____

_____

_____

_____

_____

_____

PSALM 119:89

"Forever, O LORD, thy word is settled in heaven (KJV)."

"Your eternal word, O LORD, stands firm in heaven (NLT)."

Journal Notes

_____

_____

_____

_____

_____

_____

_____

_____

_____

PSALM 119:90

"Thy faithfulness is unto all generations: thou hast established the earth, and it abideth (KJV)."

"Your faithfulness extends to every generation, as enduring as the earth you created *(NLT)."*

Journal Notes

_____

_____

_____

_____

_____

_____

_____

_____

_____

_____

PSALM 119:91

"They continue this day according to thine ordinances: for all are thy servants (KJV)."

"Your regulations remain true to this day, for everything serves your plans (NLT)."

Journal Notes

_____

_____

_____

_____

_____

_____

_____

_____

_____

_____

PSALM 119:92

"Unless thy law had been my delights, I should then have perished in mine affliction (KJV)."

"If your instructions hadn't sustained me with joy, I would have died in my misery (NLT)."

Journal Notes

_____

_____

_____

_____

_____

_____

_____

_____

_____

_____

PSALM 119:93

"I will never forget thy precepts: for with them thou hast quickened me (KJV)."

"I will never forget your commandments, for by them you give me life *(NLT)."*

Journal Notes

_____

_____

_____

_____

_____

_____

_____

_____

_____

_____

PSALM 119:94

"I am thine, save me: for I have sought thy precepts (KJV)."

"I am yours; rescue me! For I have worked hard at obeying your commandments (NLT)."

Journal Notes

_____

_____

_____

_____

_____

_____

_____

_____

_____

_____

PSALM 119:95

"The wicked have waited for me to destroy me: but I will consider thy testimonies (KJV)."

"Though the wicked hide along the way to kill me, I will quietly keep my mind on your laws (NLT)."

Journal Notes

_____

_____

_____

_____

_____

_____

_____

_____

_____

_____

PSALM 119:96

"I have seen an end of all perfection: but thy commandment is exceeding broad (KJV)."

"Even perfection has its limits, but your commands have no limit (NLT)."

Journal Notes

_____

_____

_____

_____

_____

_____

_____

_____

_____

_____

PSALM 119:97

"O how love I thy law! It is my meditation all the day (KJV)."

"Oh, how I love your instructions! I think about them all day long (NLT)."

Journal Notes

_____

_____

_____

_____

_____

_____

_____

_____

_____

_____

PSALM 119:98

"Thou through thy commandments hast made me wiser than mine enemies: for they are ever before me (KJV)."

"Your commands make me wiser than my enemies, for they are my constant guide (NLT)."

Journal Notes

_____

_____

_____

_____

_____

_____

_____

_____

_____

_____

PSALM 119:99

"I have more understanding than all my teachers: for thy testimonies are my meditation (KJV)."

"Yes, I have more insight than my teachers, for I am always thinking of your laws *(NLT)."*

Journal Notes

_____

_____

_____

_____

_____

_____

_____

_____

_____

_____

PSALM 119:100

"I understand more than the ancients, because I keep thy precepts (KJV)."

"I am even wiser than my elders, for I have kept your commandments (NLT)."

Journal Notes

_____

_____

_____

_____

_____

_____

_____

_____

_____

_____

PSALM 119:101

"I have refrained my feet from every evil way, that I might keep thy word (KJV)."

"I have refused to walk on any evil path, so that I may remain obedient to your word (NLT)."

Journal Notes

_____

_____

_____

_____

_____

_____

_____

_____

_____

_____

PSALM 119:102

"I have not departed from thy judgments: for thou hast taught me (KJV)."

"I haven't turned away from your regulations, for you have taught me well (NLT)."

<u>Journal Notes</u>

_____

_____

_____

_____

_____

_____

_____

_____

_____

_____

PSALM 119:103

"How sweet are thy words unto my taste! Yea sweeter than honey to my mouth (KJV)!"

"How sweet your words taste to me; they are sweeter than honey (NLT)."

<u>Journal Notes</u>

_____

_____

_____

_____

_____

_____

_____

_____

_____

_____

PSALM 119:104

"Through thy precepts I get understanding: therefore I hate every false way (KJV)."

"Your commandments give me understanding; no wonder I hate every false way of life (NLT)."

Journal Notes

_____

_____

_____

_____

_____

_____

_____

_____

_____

_____

PSALM 119:105

"Thy word is a lamp unto my feet, and a light unto my path (KJV)."

"Your word is a lamp to guide my feet and a light for my path (NLT)."

Journal Notes

PSALM 119:106

"I have sworn, and I will perform it, that I will keep thy righteous judgments (KJV)."

"I've promised it once, and I'll promise it again: I will obey your righteous regulations (NLT)."

Journal Notes

_____

_____

_____

_____

_____

_____

_____

_____

_____

_____

PSALM 119:107

"I am afflicted very much: quicken me, O LORD, according unto thy word (KJV)."

"I have suffered much, O LORD; restore my life again as you promised (NLT)."

Journal Notes

_____

_____

_____

_____

_____

_____

_____

_____

_____

_____

PSALM 119:108

"Accept, I beseech thee, the freewill offerings of my mouth, O LORD, and teach me thy judgments (KJV)."

"LORD, accept my offering of praise, and teach me your regulations (NLT)."

Journal Notes

_____

_____

_____

_____

_____

_____

_____

_____

_____

_____

PSALM 119:109

"My soul is continually in my hand: yet do I not forget thy law (KJV)."

"My life constantly hangs in the balance, but I will not stop obeying your instructions (NLT)."

Journal Notes

_____

_____

_____

_____

_____

_____

_____

_____

_____

_____

PSALM 119:110

"The wicked have laid a snare for me: yet I erred not from thy precepts (KJV)."

"The wicked have set their traps for me, but I will not turn from your commandments (NLT)."

Journal Notes

_____

_____

_____

_____

_____

_____

_____

_____

_____

_____

PSALM 119:111

"Thy testimonies have I taken as an heritage forever: for they are the rejoicing of my heart (KJV)."

"Your laws are my treasure; they are my heart's delight *(NLT)."*

<u>Journal Notes</u>

_____

_____

_____

_____

_____

_____

_____

_____

_____

PSALM 119:112

"I have inclined mine heart to perform thy statutes always, even unto the end (KJV)."

"I am determined to keep your decrees to the very end (NLT)."

Journal Notes

_____

_____

_____

_____

_____

_____

_____

_____

_____

_____

PSALM 119:113

"I hate vain thoughts: but thy law do I love (KJV)."

"I hate those with divided loyalties, but I love your instructions *(NLT)."*

<u>Journal Notes</u>

PSALM 119:114

"Thou are my hiding place and my shield; I hope in thy word (KJV)."

"You are my refuge and my shield; your word is my source of hope (NLT)."

Journal Notes

_____

_____

_____

_____

_____

_____

_____

_____

_____

_____

PSALM 119:115

"Depart from me, ye evildoers: for I will keep the commandments of my God (KJV)."

"Get out of my life, you evil-minded people, for I intend to obey the commands of my God (NLT)."

Journal Notes

_____

_____

_____

_____

_____

_____

_____

_____

_____

_____

PSALM 119:116

"Uphold me according unto thy word, that I may live: and let me not be ashamed of my hope (KJV)."

"LORD, sustain me as you promised, that I may live! Do not let my hope be crushed (NLT)."

Journal Notes

_____

_____

_____

_____

_____

_____

_____

_____

_____

PSALM 119:117

"Hold thou me up, and I shall be safe: and I will have respect unto thy statutes continually (KJV)."

"Sustain me, and I will be rescued; then I will meditate continually on your decrees (NLT)."

Journal Notes

_____

_____

_____

_____

_____

_____

_____

_____

_____

PSALM 119:118

"Thou hast trodden down all them that err from thy statutes: for their deceit is falsehood (KJV)."

"But you have rejected all who stray from your decrees. They are only fooling themselves (NLT)."

Journal Notes

_____

_____

_____

_____

_____

_____

_____

_____

_____

PSALM 119:119

"Thou puttest away all the wicked of the earth like dross: therefore I love thy testimonies (KJV)."

"You skim off the wicked of the earth like scum; no wonder I love to obey your laws (NLT)!"

Journal Notes

_____

_____

_____

_____

_____

_____

_____

_____

_____

_____

PSALM 119:120

"My flesh trembleth for fear of thee; and I am afraid of thy judgments (KJV)."

"I tremble in fear of you; I stand in awe of your regulations (NLT)."

Journal Notes

_____

_____

_____

_____

_____

_____

_____

_____

_____

_____

PSALM 119:121

"I have done judgment and justice: leave me not to mine oppressors (KJV)."

"Don't leave me to the mercy of my enemies, for I have done what is just and right (NLT)."

Journal Notes

_____

_____

_____

_____

_____

_____

_____

_____

_____

_____

PSALM 119:122

"Be surety for thy servant for good: let not the proud oppress me (KJV)."

"Please guarantee a blessing for me. Don't let the arrogant oppress me (NLT)!"

Journal Notes

_____

_____

_____

_____

_____

_____

_____

_____

_____

_____

PSALM 119:123

"Mine eyes fail for thy salvation, and for the word of thy righteousness (KJV)."

"My eyes strain to see your rescue, to see the truth of your promise fulfilled (NLT)."

Journal Notes

_____

_____

_____

_____

_____

_____

_____

_____

_____

_____

PSALM 119:124

"Deal with thy servant according unto thy mercy, and teach me thy statutes (KJV)."

"I am your servant; deal with me in unfailing love and teach me your decrees (NLT)."

Journal Notes

_____

_____

_____

_____

_____

_____

_____

_____

_____

_____

PSALM 119:125

"I am thy servant; give me understanding, that I may know thy testimonies (KJV)."

"Give discernment to me, your servant; then I will understand your laws (NLT)."

Journal Notes

_____

_____

_____

_____

_____

_____

_____

_____

_____

PSALM 119:126

"It is time for thee, LORD, to work: for they have made void thy law (KJV)."

"LORD, it is time for you to act, for these evil people have violated your instructions (NLT)."

Journal Notes

_____

_____

_____

_____

_____

_____

_____

_____

_____

_____

PSALM 119:127

"Therefore I love thy commandments above gold; yea, above fine gold (KJV)."

"Truly, I love your commands more than gold, even the finest gold (NLT)."

Journal Notes

_____

_____

_____

_____

_____

_____

_____

_____

_____

_____

PSALM 119:128

"Therefore I esteem all thy precepts concerning all things to be right; and I hate every false way (KJV)."

"Each of your commandments is right. That is why I hate every false way (NLT)."

Journal Notes

_____

_____

_____

_____

_____

_____

_____

_____

_____

PSALM 119:129

"Thy testimonies are wonderful: therefore doth my soul keep them (KJV)."

"Your laws are wonderful. No wonder I obey them (NLT)!"

Journal Notes

_____

_____

_____

_____

_____

_____

_____

_____

_____

PSALM 119:130

"The entrance of thy words giveth light; it giveth understanding unto the simple (KJV)."

"The teaching of your word gives light, so even the simple can understand (NLT)."

Journal Notes

_____

_____

_____

_____

_____

_____

_____

_____

_____

_____

PSALM 119:131

"I opened my mouth, and panted: for I longed for thy commandments (KJV)."

"I pant with expectation, longing for your commands (NLT)."

Journal Notes

_____

_____

_____

_____

_____

_____

_____

_____

_____

PSALM 119:132

"Look thou upon me, and be merciful unto me, as thou usest to do unto those that love thy name (KJV)."

"Come and show me your mercy, as you do for all who love your name (NLT)."

Journal Notes

_____

_____

_____

_____

_____

_____

_____

_____

_____

_____

PSALM 119:133

"Order my steps in thy word: and let not any iniquity have dominion over me (KJV)."

"Guide my steps by your word, so I will not be overcome by evil (NLT)."

Journal Notes

_____

_____

_____

_____

_____

_____

_____

_____

_____

_____

PSALM 119:134

"Deliver me from the oppression of man: so will I keep thy precepts (KJV)."

"Ransom me from the oppression of evil people; then I can obey your commandments (NLT).

Journal Notes

_____

_____

_____

_____

_____

_____

_____

_____

_____

_____

PSALM 119:135

"Make thy face to shine upon thy servant; and teach me thy statutes (KJV)."

"Look upon me with love; teach me your decrees (NLT)."

Journal Notes

_____

_____

_____

_____

_____

_____

_____

_____

_____

PSALM 119:136

"Rivers of water run down mine eyes, because they keep not thy law (KJV)."

"Rivers of tears gush from my eyes because people disobey your instructions (NLT)."

Journal Notes

_____

_____

_____

_____

_____

_____

_____

_____

_____

_____

PSALM 119:137

"Righteous art thou, O LORD, and upright are thy judgments (KJV)."

"O LORD, you are righteous, and your regulations are fair (NLT)."

<u>Journal Notes</u>

PSALM 119:138

"Thy testimonies that thou hast commanded are righteous and very faithful (KJV)."

"Your laws are perfect and completely trustworthy (NLT)."

Journal Notes

_____

_____

_____

_____

_____

_____

_____

_____

_____

_____

PSALM 119:139

"My zeal hath consumed me, because mine enemies have forgotten thy words (KJV)."

"I am overwhelmed with indignation, for my enemies have disregarded your words (NLT)."

Journal Notes

_____

_____

_____

_____

_____

_____

_____

_____

_____

_____

PSALM 119:140

"Thy word is very pure: therefore thy servant loveth it (KJV)."

"Your promises have been thoroughly tested; that is why I love them so much (NLT)."

Journal Notes

_____

_____

_____

_____

_____

_____

_____

_____

_____

_____

PSALM 119:141

"I am small and despised: yet do not I forget thy precepts (KJV)."

"I am insignificant and despised, but I don't forget your commandments (NLT)."

Journal Notes

_____

_____

_____

_____

_____

_____

_____

_____

_____

PSALM 119:142

"Thy righteousness is an everlasting righteousness, and thy law is the truth (KJV)."

"Your justice is eternal, and your instructions are perfectly true (NLT)."

Journal Notes

_____

_____

_____

_____

_____

_____

_____

_____

_____

_____

PSALM 119:143

"Trouble and anguish have taken hold on me: yet thy commandments are my delights (KJV)."

"As pressure and stress bear down on me, I find joy in your commands (NLT)."

Journal Notes

_____

_____

_____

_____

_____

_____

_____

_____

_____

_____

PSALM 119:144

"The righteousness of thy testimonies is everlasting: give me understanding, and I shall live (KJV)."

"Your laws are always right; help me to understand them so I may live (NLT)."

Journal Notes

_____

_____

_____

_____

_____

_____

_____

_____

_____

_____

PSALM 119:145

"I cried with my whole heart; hear me, O LORD: I will keep thy statutes (KJV)."

"I pray with all my heart; answer me, LORD! I will obey your decrees (NLT)."

Journal Notes

_____

_____

_____

_____

_____

_____

_____

_____

_____

_____

PSALM 119:146

"I cried unto thee; save me, and I shall keep thy testimonies (KJV)."

"I cry out to you; rescue me, that I may obey your laws (NLT)."

Journal Notes

_____

_____

_____

_____

_____

_____

_____

_____

_____

_____

PSALM 119:147

"I prevented the dawning of the morning, and cried: I hoped in thy word (KJV)."

"I rise early, before the sun is up; I cry out for help and put my hope in your words (NLT)."

Journal Notes

_____

_____

_____

_____

_____

_____

_____

_____

_____

_____

PSALM 119:148

"Mine eyes prevent the night watches, that I might meditate in thy word (KJV)."

"I stay awake through the night, thinking about your promise (NLT)."

Journal Notes

_____

_____

_____

_____

_____

_____

_____

_____

_____

_____

PSALM 119:149

"Hear my voice according unto thy lovingkindness: O LORD, quicken me according to thy judgment (KJV)."

"In your faithful love, O LORD, hear my cry; let me be revived by following your regulations (NLT)."

Journal Notes

_____

_____

_____

_____

_____

_____

_____

_____

_____

_____

PSALM 119:150

"They draw nigh that follow after mischief: they are far from thy law (KJV)."

"Lawless people are coming to attack me; they live far from your instructions (NLT)."

Journal Notes

_____

_____

_____

_____

_____

_____

_____

_____

_____

PSALM 119:151

"Thou art near, O LORD; and all thy commandments are truth (KJV)."

"But you are near, O LORD, and all your commands are true (NLT)."

Journal Notes

_____

_____

_____

_____

_____

_____

_____

_____

_____

PSALM 119:152

"Concerning thy testimonies, I have known of old that thou hast founded them forever (KJV)."

"I have known from my earliest days that your laws will last forever (NLT)."

Journal Notes

_____

_____

_____

_____

_____

_____

_____

_____

_____

_____

PSALM 119:153

"Consider mine affliction, and deliver me: for I do not forget thy law (KJV)."

"Look upon my suffering and rescue me, for I have not forgotten your instructions (NLT)."

Journal Notes

_____

_____

_____

_____

_____

_____

_____

_____

_____

_____

PSALM 119:154

"Plead my cause, and deliver me: quicken me according to thy word (KJV)."

"Argue my case; take my side! Protect my life as you promised (NLT)."

Journal Notes

_____

_____

_____

_____

_____

_____

_____

_____

_____

PSALM 119:155

"Salvation is far from the wicked: for they seek not thy statutes (KJV)."

"The wicked are far from rescue, for they do not bother with your decrees (NLT)."

Journal Notes

_____

_____

_____

_____

_____

_____

_____

_____

_____

_____

PSALM 119:156

"Great are thy tender mercies, O LORD: quicken me according to thy judgments (KJV)."

"LORD, how great is your mercy; let me be revived by following your regulations (NLT)."

Journal Notes

_____

_____

_____

_____

_____

_____

_____

_____

_____

_____

PSALM 119:157

"Many are my persecutors and mine enemies; yet do I not decline from thy testimonies (KJV)."

"Many persecute and trouble me, yet I have not swerved from your laws (NLT)."

Journal Notes

_____

_____

_____

_____

_____

_____

_____

_____

_____

_____

PSALM 119:158

"I beheld the transgressors, and was grieved; because they kept not thy word (KJV)."

"Seeing these traitors makes me sick at heart, because they care nothing for your word (NLT)."

Journal Notes

_____

_____

_____

_____

_____

_____

_____

_____

_____

PSALM 119:159

"Consider how I love thy precepts: quicken me, O LORD, according to thy lovingkindness (KJV)."

"See how I love your commandments, LORD. Give back my life because of your unfailing love (NLT)."

Journal Notes

_____

_____

_____

_____

_____

_____

_____

_____

_____

_____

_____

PSALM 119:160

"Thy word is true from the beginning: and everyone of thy righteous judgments endureth for ever (KJV)."

"The very essence of your words is truth; all your just regulations will stand forever (NLT)."

Journal Notes

_____

_____

_____

_____

_____

_____

_____

_____

_____

PSALM 119:161

"Princes have persecuted me without a cause: but my heart standeth in awe of thy word (KJV)."

"Powerful people harass me without cause, but my heart trembles only at your word (NLT)."

Journal Notes

_____

_____

_____

_____

_____

_____

_____

_____

_____

PSALM 119:162

"I rejoice at thy word, as one that findeth great spoil (KJV)."

"I rejoice in your word like one who discovers a great treasure (NLT)."

Journal Notes

_____

_____

_____

_____

_____

_____

_____

_____

_____

_____

PSALM 119:163

"I hate and abhor lying: but thy law do I love (KJV)."

"I hate and abhor all falsehood, but I love your instructions (NLT)."

Journal Notes

_____

_____

_____

_____

_____

_____

_____

_____

_____

PSALM 119:164

"Seven times a day do I praise thee because of thy righteous judgments (KJV)."

"I will praise you seven times a day because all your regulations are just (NLT)."

Journal Notes

_____

_____

_____

_____

_____

_____

_____

_____

_____

_____

PSALM 119:165

"Great peace have they which love thy law: and nothing shall offend them (KJV)."

"Those who love your instructions have great peace and do not stumble (NLT)."

Journal Notes

_____

_____

_____

_____

_____

_____

_____

_____

_____

_____

PSALM 119:166

"LORD, I have hoped for thy salvation, and done thy commandments (KJV)."

"I long for your rescue, LORD, so I have obeyed your commands (NLT)."

Journal Notes

_____

_____

_____

_____

_____

_____

_____

_____

_____

_____

PSALM 119:167

"My soul hath kept thy testimonies; and I love them exceedingly (KJV)."

"I have obeyed your laws, for I love them very much (NLT)."

Journal Notes

_____

_____

_____

_____

_____

_____

_____

_____

_____

_____

PSALM 119:168

"I have kept thy precepts and thy testimonies: for all my ways are before thee *(KJV)."*

"Yes, I obey your commandments and laws because you know everything I do *(NLT)."*

<u>Journal Notes</u>

_____

_____

_____

_____

_____

_____

_____

_____

_____

_____

PSALM 119:169

"Let my cry come near before thee, O LORD: give me understanding according to thy word (KJV)."

"O LORD, listen to my cry; give me the discerning mind you promised (NLT)."

Journal Notes

_____

_____

_____

_____

_____

_____

_____

_____

_____

_____

PSALM 119:170

"Let my supplication come before thee: deliver me according to thy word (KJV)."

"Listen to my prayer; rescue me as you promised (NLT)."

Journal Notes

_____

_____

_____

_____

_____

_____

_____

_____

_____

_____

_____

PSALM 119:171

"My lips shall utter praise, when thou hast taught me thy statutes (KJV)."

"Let praise flow from my lips, for you have taught me your decrees (NLT)."

Journal Notes

_____

_____

_____

_____

_____

_____

_____

_____

_____

_____

_____

PSALM 119:172

"My tongue shall speak of thy word: for all thy commandments are righteousness (KJV)."

"Let my tongue sing about your word, for all your commands are right (NLT)."

Journal Notes

_____

_____

_____

_____

_____

_____

_____

_____

_____

_____

_____

PSALM 119:173

"Let thine hand help me; for I have chosen thy precepts (KJV)."

"Give me a helping hand, for I have chosen to follow your commandments (NLT)."

Journal Notes

_____

_____

_____

_____

_____

_____

_____

_____

_____

_____

PSALM 119:174

"I have longed for thy salvation, O LORD; and thy law is my delight (KJV)."

"O LORD, I have longed for your rescue, and your instructions are my delight (NLT)."

<u>Journal Notes</u>

_____

_____

_____

_____

_____

_____

_____

_____

_____

_____

_____

PSALM 119:175

"Let my soul live, and it shall praise thee; and let thy judgments help me (KJV)."

"Let me live so I can praise you, and may your regulations help me (NLT)."

Journal Notes

_____

_____

_____

_____

_____

_____

_____

_____

_____

PSALM 119:176

"I have gone astray like a lost sheep; seek thy servant; for I do not forget thy commandments *(KJV)*."

"I have wandered away like a lost sheep; come and find me, for I have not forgotten your commands *(NLT)*."

Journal Notes

_____

_____

_____

_____

_____

_____

_____

_____

_____

88949324R00098

Made in the USA
Columbia, SC
14 February 2018